I Can Be Happy, Too

Dedication

To my parents,
William G. and Serena Walker,
who modeled courage, strength, grace
and a positive mental attitude during adversity.

ISBN 978-1-68192-537-0 (Inventory No. T2426)
RELIGION / Christianity / Catholic
LCCN: 2019943443

PRINTED IN THE UNITED STATES OF AMERICA

I Can Be Happy, Too

A Book about Attitudes

Text and illustrations by Susan A. Howard

When my sister takes things
without asking,
I can feel really MAD!

But I can be happy, too!

God loves a cheerful giver.
2 Corinthians 9:7

When my sister is careless
and breaks things,
I can feel woefully sad.

But I can be happy, too!

When cares increase within me,
your comfort gives me joy.
Psalm 94:19

At night when it's dark and too quiet,
I am too frightened to sleep.

But I can be happy, too!

Do not fear: I am with you;
do not be anxious: I am your God.
I will strengthen you, I will help you,
I will uphold you with my victorious right hand.
Isaiah 41:10

When bullies make fun,
taunt and tease me,
my confidence falls in a heap.

But I can be happy, too!

Blessed are they who are persecuted
for the sake of righteousness,
for theirs is the kingdom of heaven.
Matthew 5:10

When my friends aren't home
and there's nothing to do,
I can get bored and blue.

But I can be happy, too!

In all circumstances give thanks,
for this is the will of God for you in Christ Jesus.
1 Thessalonians 5:18

When something cancels
my plans for the day,
I can feel grumpy and cross.

But I can be happy, too!

**Find your delight in the Lord
who will give you your heart's desire.**
Psalm 37:4

Sometimes I think
I will always be sad,
when suffering
sickness or loss.

Mom says that
this will pass, too.

Blessed are they who mourn,
for they will be comforted.
Matthew 5:4

It isn't always easy
to control my feelings.
But as long as I can help it...
I choose to be happy!